OUTSMARTING
UNCERTAINTY

OUTSMARTING UNCERTAINTY

CREATE YOUR BEST LIFE AMID CHAOS AND ANXIETY

MARK VALENZIANO

Book design by Vinnie Kinsella, Paper Chain Book Publishing Services

ISBN: 978-1-7375244-0-3
eISBN: 978-1-7375244-1-0
LCCN: 2021914317

Note

The ideas for this book started swirling around my brain in 2017, but it is no coincidence I finally found my voice for it in 2020, a year burdened with a global pandemic, deep economic despair, and unprecedented politicization and division. This writing is not born of public health, political, and social justice challenges, but it will help you move through them.

These types of issues did not go away with the flip of the calendar to 2021, and even as some things start to normalize, as a global society, we've started down a new path that will require some navigation. With this book, I suggest you make small decisions that will lessen your feelings of doubt and hesitancy and restore calm, focus, confidence—restore happiness!—to your life. Stop watching, reading, or listening to the news, or at least greatly reduce the frequency with which you consume news. Put your energy on things that make you feel good: crafts, art, writing, reading (not of the news!), exercise, learning. Communicate with friends so you know you're not alone. Find small goals within your life. If you're distracted at work, then choose a small work project and get it done. Focusing on things within your control will help reduce your feelings of helplessness.

Things will get better, but until then, rinse and repeat.

Okay, let's get on with outsmarting uncertainty!

Preview

Introduction

Uncertainty can lead to stress, worry, and doubt. Uncertainty can lead to feelings of inadequacy and insecurity. Uncertainty can stifle your progress in personal, professional, and organizational development. But what if you could look at uncertainty differently and turn it to your advantage?

Uncertainty can be an empowering tool that inspires and propels you forward, helping you stay motivated and driven. It can be a benchmark indicating where you are and bring direction to where you want to be. When you take charge of uncertainty, you bring balance and composure to your life. When you outsmart it, you find yourself focusing on improvement, accomplishment, and happiness. Outsmarting uncertainty is an ongoing attitude and process. You might even call it a lifestyle. This book helps you start to embody that lifestyle, highlighting the powers of acceptance, social intelligence, purpose, and resilience. It introduces ways to let uncertainty help you take more charge, enjoy more success, and be undeterred by uncertainty.

Later I will introduce my Balanced-Uncertainty Index. You will understand the Uncertainty Sweet Spot is not living in complete certainty. This index asks questions that measure your level of worry or discomfort with general areas of your life. The gap between your answers and the Sweet Spot is your personal opportunity for development and growth.

Let's first put uncertainty into perspective. There are what I call global, or distant, uncertainties over which you have little or no immediately impactful control. You could spend your time and energy worrying about the actions of our world leaders. You might be worrying about the future in terms of climate change, world peace, the US stock market and economy, or the debris and micro-plastics in the Great Pacific Garbage Patch.

Unequivocally, these are valid and important issues. I am not saying you should be disinterested or not participate in conversations, solutions, or elections. You should! But if you are not going to get actively involved in these sorts of big issues, then I suggest you don't spend your limited energy worrying about them. If you are not working within one of these silos, you cannot personally control the outcome of the uncertainty. Stay aware and be knowledgeable, but don't fixate. When a person spends too much of their "worry energy" on the distant uncertainties, they may be filling their life with anxiety and even become distraught. Too much anxiousness and distress can result in stagnation. We each have a finite amount of energy to spend. The first step in outsmarting uncertainty is to accept that premise and to focus your energy on the uncertainties closer to home, the ones over which you have more immediate control. In fact, this book will even encourage you to create some uncertainties in your life. We all need a balanced level of uncertainty and vulnerability to keep us inquisitive, creative, and moving forward. In areas of management, teamwork, personal development, and relationships, absolute certainty may mean you are closed-minded and lacking curiosity, vulnerability, and creativity. This might mean you are rigid and even a bit dictatorial.

When there is uncertainty, leadership becomes crucial. We look to our leaders for guidance, direction, and confidence during times of uncertainty or uncertain situations. Whether they are community leaders, political leaders, business leaders and bosses, or parents or spouses, we look to them to be our beacons. You can tell from that list that we are all leaders, whether it is of only ourselves or of teams of hundreds. Leading through times of high uncertainty is difficult. Our social, family, and work lives can be flipped upside down. In organizations, operations and decisions are more challenging and carry more risk. In some cases, plans and strategies are completely tossed out, and you might feel as if you're starting over. But leadership is still required.

So, leading through times of high uncertainty is your opportunity to exhibit compassion, empathy, and confidence—toward yourself and others. These important elements of leadership will calm nerves and coalesce your team. When you raise up the sights, achievements, confidence, optimism, and happiness of the individuals, the success of the whole is elevated.

This unique look at uncertainty can be a new growth frontier for you, personally and professionally. This book will help put you in charge of your future, resulting in more accomplishments, less worry, and more happiness.

Please think about your future as any moment in time after this very moment right now. It can be a few hours, days, weeks, months, or years from now. Too often people think about the future as a distant point hovering over the horizon, and they fail to give it any attention since it seems so far away. To help you face a front-and-center future, this book also introduces the Pillars of Strength that I have found fuel my resilience no matter what life throws at me. Each of our lives is its own unique journey, but one thing we have in common is that journey is often along bumpy roads. Let's face it—life is difficult and can sometimes be downright cruel. Without these pillars to lean on, it could be easy to stumble.

Although the backdrop for this book is stories and insights from my life filled with uncertainty due to challenges, change, adversity, and transformation, this book is about you. It's about getting you to think differently: about the world, about your future, about you. It's about what I call the inner movie, you writing, directing, starring in, and producing your perfect life. Reflection is a personal thing, so, executive or administrative, wealthy or wanting, this "you" I'm talking to is, truly, you, no matter who you are or want to be.

How will you turn change and uncertainty to your advantage? The dynamic nature of life makes them unavoidable, so how will you embrace them and gain strength from them?

Reading these words, are you starting to feel a bit of tension in your shoulders or gut? Do you tend to avoid, resist, or even fear change? Let's think about this for a moment. Whether you realize it all the time or not, you've been successfully adapting and progressing all your life, and you are better because of it. You can't honestly say you are the exact same person you were two, five, or ten years ago, can you? You might not be exactly who you want to be at this moment, but this book will help you get yourself there.

Having the ability to thrive through all types of change and uncertainty is integral to staying grounded and happy. One way to thrive through change is to always stay a step ahead. Let's start by looking each type of change in the face.

Generally, there are three types of change we encounter throughout life:

- Change that is thrust upon us and is often unwanted
- Change that naturally occurs throughout life
- Change that we desire and initiate

Change that is thrust upon us includes accidents, injuries, and illness and divorce or unemployment, your own or for loved ones. Often, this kind of change is difficult and trying. It alters our mood. Our outlook. And if we're not careful, it will change the course of our life. We may not possess control to halt, reverse, or avoid these situations and their accompanying uncertainty, but we own the power to control how we respond. How we react. And how we move forward in a positive way. We own the power to be resilient. It is okay to want happiness. It is okay to move forward, evolve, and grow. If a dark cloud hangs just above you, brought on by events such as the death of a loved one, the unwanted ending of a personal or professional relationship, or unexpected financial strain, be kind and compassionate to yourself. Give yourself permission to grieve and feel the pain. Give yourself permission to look to the future and give yourself permission to be happy.

Change that occurs over time is inevitable. Friends and neighbors move in and out of our lives. Jobs change. Our political leaders change; some we like, and some we don't. Marriage. Births. Disappointments. Victories. We make money. We lose money. Our youthful agility is replaced with aches and pains. It's all part of life. But again, we possess the power to control how we respond. How we react.

And then there is the change that we seek. That we desire. That we initiate and implement. I like to think of this transformation as development and growth. And although change often carries uncertainty and trepidation with it, this type of change is backed with excitement and enthusiasm. Even when this change is extraordinarily difficult, like kicking a bad habit out of your life, I urge you to consider the process of change as a positive step forward in your life. With each step you take, let more and more of your resistance melt away.

Your first challenge is to get your head right! Do you consider yourself flexible, adaptable, and open to change?

Or are you more of the rigid type who is resistant? For the rest of this short book to have any impact on you personally, you need to see yourself as open to change. Adaptable. If this does not come easily for you, I suggest you do this simple exercise for one minute: Sit comfortably and close your eyes. Conjure up a good image of your face. Picture yourself with a big, proud smile. Feel the sense of pride and satisfaction from accomplishment. Know that you have the power to be flexible and adaptable. Think, *I can take on the challenge of change. I'm adaptable. I got this.* For the remainder of this book, keep seeing yourself as adaptable and flexible. Keep this picture of yourself in mind, and let's get started!

SCENE 2

The Powerful Source
of Freedom Within You

Acceptance is far more freeing and empowering than denial or resistance are. When we do not have the power to change a situation or extricate ourselves from it, then our best alternative is to accept it and focus our positive energy on things we can control. Life is filled with those uncertainties you cannot control or change. Learn to accept them, so you can prepare accordingly rather than worry.

I was first confronted with this concept at the age of fifteen, when I was told I was going blind. It was a sunny spring day. I was enjoying a normal day at school. Or so I thought.

I was new at the high school in Warren, New Jersey. We had moved just in time for me to start freshman year. Making friends was going well, and I was settling in. This day was going fine, until seventh-period band class. I was a drummer, and from my perch on the top tier of the large band room, I could see down over lots of musicians and to the conductor front and center. In the middle of a song, with no notice whatsoever, I went completely blind. In an instant, my world went dark. I had no idea what was happening. I was terrified, and dizzy. Running my left hand against the back wall to guide me, I made it to a small room in the corner, where I collapsed to the floor, trembling and crying.

Later that day, Dr. Paul Ocken explained the cause of the sudden and complete blindness and assured me my sight would return, although only temporarily. During his exam, he noticed spots on my retinas and had the unfortunate task of telling me I had a rare disease that would ultimately render me blind. What does a teenage kid do with that news?

For the next few months, we traipsed from doctor to doctor in hopes of hearing something different. The specialists in New Jersey, New York, and Boston all concurred with Dr. Ocken's diagnosis. And there was no treatment or cure.

I was fifteen. I wanted to be thinking about girls and cars. Instead, I was grappling with the concept of permanent darkness. Like being pummeled off-balance by a rapid succession of ocean waves breaking against me, I was quickly becoming more and more aware of all the aspects of my life that would change. That would be different. What about reading, which I loved to do? Would I finish high school on time with my friends? What about going to college…having a career…getting around…living independently…getting married…having a family…?

The uncertainty of my future was overwhelming, and I was scared and anxious.

I could not change the fact I had this disease. I was going

blind. To help clear the fog, something else had to change, and it was me. I was at a fork in the road. My life was not going to continue as it had been. Now it was a matter of me choosing the direction my life would take. I may not be able to change the medical situation, but I realized I could still be in control of my future. I would control how I reacted.

Truly accepting my situation took a few months. But after a while of feeling dazed and sorry for myself, here's what I did: I started to literally see myself differently!

I found myself in a movie theater, paying little attention to the movie. Instead, I was imagining myself up on that big screen. There I was, a teenage boy who had recently been told he was going blind. How would that kid on the screen react to this news? What would the next scene of this movie be? How would his story unfold?

How was I going to react? How was my life going to unfold?

Hey, someone writes the script for each movie we see. Someone is thinking far and not so far into the future and determining the characters' storylines. Why couldn't I do that for the most important storyline: my life?

Right then and there, it was born: the tool I would use to guide me through life's situations—large and small. The tool I would use to help me take my life to where I wanted it to go.

I call it my inner movie, and I get to write, direct, and star in every one of its next scenes.

This thought excited me. I started feeling like I had some control amid a scary situation and massive uncertainty. Turns out I was right.

When I truly accepted my situation, my thoughts and energy naturally shifted from stifling worry and anxiety to preparation and action.

Now I use my inner movie often in many parts of my life. It's a way of thinking forward and determining the result I desire and the best course of action to achieve that result. It is something I use far more than just in times of high anxiety. Pick anything in your life and decide your goal for it. Maybe it's the kind of wedding you want or that promotion you're seeking at work. Maybe it's how you're going to successfully deal with something challenging in your life. Whatever it is, your inner movie is a powerful tool immediately available to you.

Reflection Question

What are two or three things in your life over which you have no control but you worry about? Jot them down.

Accept these as part of your world. Shift your energy to issues, goals, and changes over which you have a level of control.

I'm not very religious, but the words of the Serenity Prayer apply here beautifully:

"God, grant me the serenity to accept the things I cannot change, courage to change the things I can, and wisdom to know the difference."

SCENE 3

Maximized Social Intelligence Minimizes Uncertainty

S ocial intelligence is crucial to getting what you want: that is, a handle on uncertainty.

Early in my journey from sighted to blind, I realized I'd need lots of help, and I'd need strong relationships to build the life I wanted. I need people. We all need people.

Fundamentally, social intelligence is your capability to understand your human environment, adapt accordingly, and react consistently and appropriately for socially successful interactions, all while maintaining your sense of self.

Generally, social intelligence encompasses self-awareness, external awareness, and language. People with good self-identity and strong social skills are best prepared to accomplish their dreams and goals. The ability to communicate productively is a key contributor to happiness.

Self-Awareness

It all starts with you! Who are you? To react consistently to life's challenges, you first must be comfortable and grounded with yourself. Take a good long look at yourself up on your imaginary movie screen. What do you see? Where are you in life? With whom have you surrounded yourself? Are you who you want to be? Knowing who you are will help you find direction in life and help you stand steadfast in the face of life's uncertainties.

Great self-awareness is bringing your life and your future into clear focus. This includes your goals and dreams and aspirations. Your words and behaviors. And even your flaws and insecurities. It's knowing your values and what you stand for.

And it's having a clear and honest picture of who you are today and who you want to be tomorrow.

While sitting in that movie theater as a teenager, I rolled my inner movie and looked far into my future and decided what kind of person I wanted to be. What kind of blind person I would become. Who I wanted to figuratively "see" in the mirror. I envisioned myself as an optimistic person who was not going to use this eyesight thing as a crutch or excuse. I pictured myself at different ages to imprint my mind with the image of myself feeling happy and optimistic. I tried to feel (this word is key, as I'll soon explain) those difficult milestones in my life when my sight would disappear rapidly for a few months before plateauing for another unknown stretch of time, as the doctor had explained. I determined how I'd generally behave during these periods when I'd be losing more than just precious eyesight; independence and other abilities would be slipping away as well.

I was too young to know what I wanted to do in life, but I did have a good picture of the kind of person I wanted to be. I wanted to outweigh the help I needed with the help I gave. I wanted to authentically behave in a way that immediately converted people's feelings of sympathy for me into inspiration for themselves. Among my friends and community, I wanted to be considered a beacon of strength. And I began to see that distant future as a present one too; I pictured the next few weeks and months of my future to determine my attitude, behavior, and demeanor amid processing the news of my disease, creating a strong present that would be a foundation for the far-off future.

Hands down, those couple of hours in the movie theater imagining my future and becoming self-aware are the most important and formative hours of my life. I walked into that theater as a little boy with an eye disease. I walked out as a young man with a vision.

Your storyline is the narrative of your life. All the connected events that have occurred. Your decisions. And so much of that is still in front of you!

Do you have that good and honest picture of the person you want to be? Are you directing your life or playing a cameo role and just letting life happen to you?

Your future is not just that distant moment hovering at the horizon. "Future" is any moment after this moment right now. It might be the important telephone conversation you're having later today. Or the sales presentation you're giving next week. Or the speech you're giving in two months. You might be picturing yourself as a newlywed or first-time parent. Maybe you're picturing how you'll feel when you get that promotion or achieve some other special goal. No matter what or when it is, employ your brain to maximize self-awareness and visualize your desired outcome.

What do you want out of that phone conversation, and how will you achieve it? Who will be in that sales presentation, and what questions will they have? How do you want the audience to feel and respond at the end of your speech? What kind of spouse or parent do you want to be? How will you feel when you get that degree or promotion or finish that half-marathon? Or maybe you're picturing yourself not smoking anymore or having lost those pesky thirteen pounds.

Whatever it is, decide how you want to feel and picture yourself feeling that way. Before I take on a challenge, step on a stage, or enter a meeting, I envision how I want to feel when it's over. Keeping that final scene in mind is critical to success and helps me design my road map to getting there.

Engage your imagination. Just how a Major League batter anticipates the pitcher's throw and visualizes hitting the ball or how an NFL receiver visualizes catching the ball amid attacking defenders, you too can use your imagination to visualize the outcomes you desire. Decide what quantifiable or emotional outcome you seek and then visualize how you want to feel when you achieve those results. It's always easier to achieve your dreams and goals if you first visualize them.

No matter how far forward in time you are thinking—days, weeks, months, or years—always keep your future in mind as you make today's decisions. But never forget that you only have control over one thing: what you say or do in this one moment. Thankfully, we can act in this present moment for a goal for the future. So, make today's words, actions, and decisions consistent with who you want to be or what you want to achieve tomorrow. The future is inside of us, not in front of us. Today's thoughts, actions, and decisions become tomorrow's realities.

By using your inner movie to think through your goal and path to getting there, you are able to identify knowledge and tools you will need to acquire, relationships you'll want to build, risks you'll want to monitor, and obstacles you may encounter. This enables you to make meaningful decisions along the way and keeps you a step ahead, and outsmarting uncertainty. Keen self-awareness also helps you recognize when your life is getting off course. We sometimes need to adjust to be the person we want to be.

In general, I picture myself as an easygoing guy, and I don't like it when I get angry. But losing your sight is hard and frustrating. And what often pushes that frustration to the forefront of anger is when you walk into something and hurt yourself. Countless times I have badly bruised my shins, knees, and shoulders. And multiple times, I've bruised and even cut up my face. For the longest time, this frustration would get the better of me, and I'd spontaneously combust, punching a wall or slamming my hand down on an unforgiving surface.

This behavior was not consistent with how I pictured myself—chill, cool, collected. I did not want to be the person who angrily exploded. This behavior bothered me greatly, and I know it pained my wife. Something had to change.

My actions were not congruent with who I wanted to be. My life was off track, and I needed to get it back on course.

So, I rolled my inner movie. I saw myself losing my temper, punching a wall, or hurting my hand as I slammed the granite countertop. And then I used my inner movie to picture myself differently and wrote a more positive script for these situations. Rather than getting angry when I hurt myself walking into something, I envisioned myself pausing quietly. Closing my eyes and biting my lip in acknowledgment of the pain and frustration. Then issuing an almost imperceptible smile to myself that silently reminds me that this is part of my journey and to simply move on.

Being honest about who I was being and having the clear picture of who I want to be made it easy to realize my behavior was off track. Without that self-awareness, the angry and somewhat violent behavior may have continued, probably resulting in negative consequences in my marriage, in how others viewed me, and in how I viewed myself.

I continue to walk into things and still sometimes hurt myself, but now my response is quite different. Using my inner movie to visualize a different response enabled me to change that behavior. I improved my happiness and my life by literally seeing myself differently and no longer expecting myself to burst with anger.

We all have an inner movie. It's just a matter of, do you use it or not? We all have behaviors we want to increase or eliminate. Sometimes we simply need to change what we have come to expect from ourselves. Over time our behaviors can become habitual and even define us. We start to think of them as "Well, that's just who I am." We just expect ourselves to behave that way.

"I've always been a procrastinator."

"I'm a smoker because I've always been a smoker."

"I've always been twenty pounds overweight; that's just who I am."

"I'm always late. I always have been."

These definitions of self are common, and here's a real-life story about that last one. There's a group of women who go to breakfast together monthly and have been doing so for years. One of the women is habitually fifteen minutes late and starts her morning greeting with an apology as she slips into the booth.

One of the other women, a friend of mine, inquired, "When you are getting ready to come meet us and looking in the mirror, do you envision yourself being late?" The response was "Yes, I do." The inquiring woman suggested that next time she picture herself differently. She said, "Next month, try picturing yourself arriving first and greeting us already seated in the booth with a smile on your face and coffee in hand."

A few weeks later, my friend got a text from the habitually tardy person that said, "Meeting my sister for lunch. Am early." And the following month at their breakfast gathering, she was in the booth early with a smile on her face and a coffee in hand!

She had simply come to expect that behavior of being late from herself. That was how she saw herself—as the friend who was always late. This was not a behavior she particularly liked. She changed her behavior by seeing herself differently. She changed what she had come to expect from herself by rolling her inner movie and envisioning different behavior. By starting to literally view herself differently, she got back in line with who she wanted to be, and she greatly increased her happiness by doing so. She gave herself permission to change. You can do the same.

We all have behaviors we'd like to modify.

Do you have a good, honest, and clear picture of who you are today and who you want to be tomorrow?

Exercise

Jot down one behavior you'd like to modify.

Then jot down the goal this change would help you achieve or the benefit it would bring to your life.

For example, an audience member at one of my presentations told me the behavior he wanted to minimize or eliminate was getting angry quickly with his kids, and his goal with this modification was to parent in a more positive manner.

We all have behaviors we want to increase or eliminate. Your inner movie is a powerful tool that can help you replace anxiety with accomplishment, as you design and create your best future amid the chaos of life.

Reflection Question

In striving to become the person you want to be, in which of these general areas of your life can you imagine setting goals and making improvements or other changes?

Personal health
Personal finances
Personal relationships
Job performance
Job level and professional advancement
Work relationships
Community involvement
Lifelong learning
Volunteerism/Charity/Philanthropy
Spirituality
Other (Jot it down!)

Strong self-identity anchors how you perceive your environment. This steadiness provides consistency in how you adapt and react in pursuit of successful social interactions. A successful social interaction is not about "winning" but rather about building. Building relationships, specifically. No matter whether with a new acquaintance or a lifelong friend, relationships of all sorts are important to mitigating uncertainty.

External Awareness

The second part of social intelligence is being acutely aware of the people around you. Being alert and attentive to their personalities, their moods, and their roles and always remembering other things that you do not know are going on in their lives. The more we recognize about the people around us, the more able we are to show compassion and empathy.

Connectiveness resides within this capacity to understand and feel what another person is experiencing. The capacity to place oneself in another's position. Care is deepened, and relationships are made more meaningful. Showing this kind of sensitivity and understanding builds trust. And times of high uncertainty require new and higher forms of trust be built.

Whether in business, community, or family, these times are opportunities for you to shine as the leader you are! Make yourself open and vulnerable so the people around you are comfortable coming to you with their needs, troubles, ideas, and questions. Be bighearted, not narrow-minded.

When you open all your senses, you will be amazed at how much you increase your awareness of everything around you. Being able to notice small details broadens your mind and improves your instincts and intuition, which improves your ability to anticipate. When you are better able to anticipate others' actions and reactions, then you are better prepared to react or respond yourself. Being better able to anticipate means you are reducing uncertainty and are more prepared to achieve the social outcome you desire.

The more awareness we have, the more social intelligence we can apply. In terms of awareness, you might think you're observing everything you can, but neural cognitive research out of NYU helps to quantify our room for improvement. The research indicates that, through your eyes alone, ten thousand bits of information are delivered to your brain every second, but you only convert one hundred of those into conscious perception. (I learned that bit of information from the excellent book *Blue Mind: The Surprising Science That Shows How Being Near, In, On, or Under Water Can Make You Happier, Healthier, More Connected, and Better at What You Do*. Author Wallace Nichols didn't conduct the research, but his book helped me explore it relative to lessening uncertainty.)

Remember, information is being delivered to our brain via all our senses. We just need to learn to recognize more of it. Eyesight is great, but don't let it blind you from all the other information you can pick up through your ears. While in your home, at your office, or in a cafe, close your eyes for one minute and listen intently to everything around you. Hear all the voices. What moods or emotions are you hearing? Are the people nearby smiling, or are they serious? What else are you hearing? How many people are typing on a keyboard or talking on their phone? Is a fork hitting a plate? Is the plate empty? Is there music playing in the background? Is someone outside mowing the lawn or blowing the leaves? Did a vehicle just go by? Listen hard. Identify every little sound in your environment. It's amazing how much one can observe about the people around them by just listening. Attention. Curiousness. Mood. Dissent. Distraction. Even facial expressions. And you don't need to lose your eyesight to increase your awareness. Just exercise your mind. Open your mind's eye and listen to all your senses and even your gut feelings.

Your inner movie is all about thinking forward, being aware, anticipating, and staying prepared. I've used my inner movie and keen external awareness to successfully launch important changes in my life. Whether it was before walking away from driving, buying out my business partners, or deciding to sell my company, I rolled my inner movie to think through all elements of the situation. This enabled me to fully anticipate and prepare. Sharpening your ability to anticipate will always be a key ingredient in success.

Foresight is defined as care or provision for the future. Prudence. The act of looking forward. Knowledge or insight gained by looking forward. A view of the future. Using your inner movie in great detail gives you the advantage of vivid foresight.

"A key element of success is self-confidence. A key element of self-confidence is preparation."

—Arthur Ashe

But don't be blind to the fact that no matter how much preparation you do, life has its way of trying to knock you off course. In 2002 my sight was disappearing quickly, and my optimistic spirit was dwindling with it. To help me cling to the tiny bit of remaining central vision I used for reading, I begrudgingly purchased my first piece of assistive technology. It was a bulky camera that hung in front of me, pointed down at printed material, and displayed the magnified text on a giant Sony TV that occupied a third of my desk. When the three big boxes arrived, it was so disheartening I could not touch them. I just left them on the living room floor.

I needed a plan to integrate this damn thing into my life. I decided to do something adventurous and exciting and for which I'd need to use this new technology to help me put my plan in motion.

So, I started planning a solo backpacking trip in the mountains of Montana. Yes, as a guy with very little eyesight, I happened to think being alone in the backwoods was a great idea! Being alone in the wilderness would be good for my soul, and a successful journey would help restore my positive outlook and optimism. I ordered my maps to plot out and memorize my trek and purchased books to remind me how to deal with bears and other daunting wildlife. I loved camping and backpacking and was excited about this idea. It was going to be a good way to start assimilating the assistive technology into my life. I wouldn't be able to read a map, or anything, for that matter, once I left my house. So, I had to use the new camera system ahead of time.

I shipped my gear to Bozeman and boarded my flight. The only assistance I sought was a driver to take me to the trailhead and pick me up five days later. Even though it was mid-June, deep snow still covered the top quarter of the mountains. Concerned the high-altitude pass would be too dangerous to attempt alone, I asked the driver to pick me up one day earlier.

As I started up the trailhead and the driver's car pulled away, I had a definite knot in my stomach. Anxiety, I guessed, fueled by being alone in the mountains to take on the demons of going blind. My goal was to straighten out my attitude and emotions and emerge from the mountains standing tall and feeling strong.

I hiked up to about eight thousand feet and set up camp just shy of the snow line, tucked between a few trees at the edge of a flowering meadow and next to a mountain stream and pine forest. Glorious.

The knot in my stomach persisted. Barely noticeable, but it was there.

Space and weight are two big concerns when packing for a trip like this. You want everything to be as small and light as possible. I had some of the best and lightest gear, and my food was all portioned out per day. On day two, I realized I'd been eating only about half my allotted rations. This was uncommon for me—especially while hiking in the mountains. I had to acknowledge the slight twinges I had been feeling in my stomach. They were growing into aches.

My last day arrived, and I packed up and headed down to the trailhead to meet my ride. The following day, Monday, I took myself on a ten-mile urban hike around the hills of beautiful Bozeman. The stomach discomfort was still present and seemed to be worsening.

Monday night I could not sleep at all. Tuesday morning I could barely choke down a piece of toast for breakfast. I called my wife in Minneapolis and told her I wasn't feeling well and was going to nap. After tossing and turning for an hour, I asked the hotel owner where the local hospital was located. I had a flight home the next morning and didn't want to fly with this mild, but odd, discomfort in my abdomen. The owner of the small hotel was so kind; she dropped everything and drove me to the hospital.

I walked into the emergency room and casually explained what I was feeling. The ER doctor examined me, made some comments, and said she wanted a surgeon to look. The surgeon did his exam and ordered a CT scan of my abdomen.

Well, here's a thing I could never have anticipated or planned for. The scan showed I had a burst appendix, and in less than an hour, I was in the operating room with a seven-inch incision down my belly. The surgeon thought it had burst a few days before. I didn't experience the sudden and acute pain that's typical because I had what's called a retrocecal appendicitis where the appendix is oddly flipped up and tucked behind the intestines, restricting the seepage of the toxic poison that causes the acute pain normally associated with appendicitis. The mild but increasing discomfort I was feeling was the poison slowly seeping out from behind the intestine.

The next day, the surgeon told me I was one of the luckiest people he'd ever met. Here are a few thoughts:

Thank goodness the snow prohibited me from trekking the full five days. It is quite possible I would have died in the backwoods, alone and in great pain.

I've always believed in Freud's theory of determinism, which states everything happens for a reason.

It is impossible to prepare so much that you remove all uncertainty from your life, but by having great awareness and making prudent decisions, you can keep uncertainty at bay.

My wife flew out to be with me. After a few days recovering in the hospital and a few more resting in the hotel, we flew home to Minneapolis where a good friend commented that my trip didn't go all that well. To the contrary, my friend; it could not have gone any better.

I went to contemplate my life as I transitioned to blindness and had this life-threatening curve ball hurled my way. My awareness and prudence helped me deal with it just fine. My mom was right when she commented that I went to the mountains to refortify my soul. I emerged with my positive attitude, optimism, and mental toughness restored. I use my inner movie to see and be the person I choose to be. Optimistic. Grateful. Happy. Successful. And my time in the mountains helped me bring it all back in to focus amid the new sets of challenges of going blind.

Unexpected challenges of all kinds are going to pop up

in your life. Stay tethered to who you are, be aware, and implement smart decisions, and you will make it through.

I've got one more reason external awareness can help us mitigate uncertainty. Connected with altruism, it can offer us relationships that steady us. A keen and caring external awareness can make you a little angel. For many people, asking for help is difficult. As awareness of your human environment grows, you may observe people who could use a few moments of your assistance. If it doesn't come naturally, I encourage you to step out of your comfort zone and offer your help. A little altruism goes a long way. I know this firsthand.

It was November, and I was in New York City to give two speeches over a few days. After my first event, which was in Queens and ended in late afternoon, I was meeting an old college friend for drinks at his office building in Manhattan. It was dark and raining when the person driving me accidentally left me at the wrong building, which I did not realize until he was long gone. With my computer pack over my shoulder, cane in hand, and only a sport coat for warmth over my dress clothes, I set out to find my way. I spoke the address into my iPhone, but I did not know exactly where I was standing or which way I was pointed, so the directions made no sense. I did not know if I should cross the street straight ahead, cross the street to my left, turn around, or take a right. I could not read any signs, and my phone was not accurately telling me where I was. The rain was steady as I stood at the curb deciding what to do. Many dozens of people hurriedly walked by, but I felt so completely alone and invisible. Until, after the light cycled green, yellow, red many times, a little angel showed up on my right. Without urgency in her voice and without startling me by grabbing my arm or cane, she simply said, "Could you use some help?"

I was so relieved to hear her kind voice! You might think this sounds minor, but imagine being alone in the middle of Manhattan on a chilly, rainy night, unable to see and having no idea which direction to turn.

I thanked her emphatically and told her where I was headed. She said she needed to get to her bank before it closed in fifteen minutes, and did I mind walking there with her first and then she'd get me to where I needed to go in Rockefeller Center? She was a musician from San Diego and was in New York to sing opera. How cool is that? It was my pleasure to escort her to her bank, which unfortunately was already closed. Her time standing at the curb talking with me was most likely the difference between her making it there in time and not. Selfless.

We were complete strangers who enjoyed good conversation while we zigged and zagged to my destination. Then we traded names, hugged, and went our own ways.

She was truly a little angel at exactly the moment I needed one. I remembered her name, Nina, and after I returned home, I Googled her and sent her an email expressing my gratitude. My message was simple: "You have no idea how much our 15-minute friendship meant to me. Thank you!"

Her awareness drew her to me, and asking if she could be of help came naturally to her. We should all call on our altruistic self to more often query others about help they might need.

It is completely fine to ask someone if they want help. They may say no, and I hope they do so with grace and gratitude. But some people have crappy attitudes and may not show grace or gratitude when rejecting your offer to help. Please do not let this dissuade you from offering your assistance to someone else down the road. They might say yes, and you may be a little angel for them as Nina was for me. Do not underestimate the immense value your tiny doses of altruism can give to this world.

Language

Along with self-awareness and external awareness, the third leg that elevates our social intelligence is language; it is what we use to mediate our interpersonal relationships.

Our words matter. We display who we are in how we act toward others. How we approach someone often determines who they become in our eyes and how they treat us in return. The extraordinary, innovative educator Ron Clark said it best, "Who we are is how we treat people. We are defined by our interactions."

Our words are the lens through which people view us. Our words are what people use to decide if they like us, want to help us, or want to do business with us. The words we deliver, and actions we take alongside those words, are quick decisions we make all day long, mostly subconsciously, in our interactions with other people. Whether it's in person, by phone, or in the written word—both digital and old-school—we decide on the words we're going to use, the attitude we're going to exhibit, and the tone we're going to take. We make these decisions so frequently and quickly that they often go overlooked. This can lead to unintended negative consequences.

At its very basic, this part of social intelligence is knowing what to say, when to say it, and how to say it.

Dale Carnegie's famous book *How to Win Friends & Influence People* is very much about this topic, teaching practical social rules like: don't criticize, condemn, or complain; encourage others to talk about themselves; show respect for other's opinions; and when we're wrong, we should admit it quickly and emphatically.

Just as important as knowing what to say and when to say it is knowing what not to say. If you are about to criticize someone, first ask yourself if your comments will help them. If you are not sure, then keep your criticism to yourself. The unintended consequence of voicing your opinion could harm that relationship. You may have strong opinions, but you do not need to share them at every opportunity. Giving your unsolicited advice makes you annoying. And are you always correcting people? If so, that makes you annoying too. By always giving unsolicited advice and correcting people, the implication is that you feel that you are somehow above them.

So often, when we are tied to our opinions, we are truly being closed-minded and not willing to hear or consider anyone else's thoughts or opinions. All too often American politics is at the heart of this stubborn righteousness. If people want to become more united, then we need to step down from our soapboxes and let in a bit more uncertainty by listening, considering, and conversing.

It all sounds so simple—knowing what to say and when to say it or knowing when to just shut up—but applying this takes great awareness and discipline. We've all been in that situation where we can't stop ourselves from saying what our emotions or ego want us to say. Maybe it's snapping at someone or being selfish. Or maybe escalating an argument simply because of the need to feel right.

Being socially intelligent is crucial for genuine authentic happiness. As busy members of the community—especially you parents—you may be under pressure and may have a lot of people making demands of you. It takes discipline, but remember that in every situation, large or small, your words and actions do really matter. When you are interacting with your six-year-old or teenager, your words always matter. When you are talking with a fellow employee, client, or supplier, your words always matter. When you are talking to a neighbor or other community member, your words always matter. Even when it's done quickly on the fly, think through the interaction. Decide how you want to feel at the end of it. Maybe more importantly, decide how you want the other person to feel. Then select your words, tone, and attitude accordingly to achieve the most successful social outcome. Your language, both verbal and nonverbal, is the most outwardly visible piece of your social intelligence. It is what people hear and observe. It is the essence of how you react to others, and it shapes how others respond to you. This makes language—and also communication overall, which includes words and actions—possibly the most important element of social intelligence and for building the many relationships required to keep uncertainty at bay.

Reflection Question

Which part or parts of your social intelligence need your attention?

Self-awareness

External awareness

Language

Spend a moment contemplating this.

SCENE 4

Build Your Pillars of Strength!

The ability to roll with uncertainty leads to happiness. But happiness does not stand alone. Happiness requires resilience. And resilience requires strength.

Let's face it, life is difficult and can sometimes be downright cruel. The uncertainties and challenges of life will periodically knock us down. The key is getting back up and standing tall as you look to your future with fortitude.

After many years of being told I'm resilient, I decided to examine my life to understand the source of that strength. I mentally reviewed the most difficult times in my life and realized that three attitudinal pillars help me stand steadfast in the face of life's challenges and uncertainties.

Resilience is a form of internal, enduring strength. It's having the will and determination to keep moving forward into your future. Resilience is having the attitude that says, "Okay, life, that was a pretty good punch. But I'm getting right back up and emerging even better!" Be resilient, no matter what. It takes mental toughness, which you have. And when you doubt your mental toughness or confidence, close your eyes and use your inner movie to see yourself being confident and mentally tough.

Having the image of you in the future—the kind of person you want to be and what you want to accomplish—will help fuel your determination. But that image alone is not enough. You need a support system on which you can lean. A support system not of just the people around you but of your own thoughts, beliefs, and attitudes—your Pillars of Strength.

I think of these attitudinal pillars not only as things to prop me up but as guideposts to keep my life on course as I navigate forward through time. They help guide my behaviors, which is especially meaningful during the turbulent times of life. They nourish my resilience. They truly hold me up when life tries to knock me down.

First is gratitude.

Gratitude is the cornerstone of happiness, and happiness is the foundation on which you build your success. Let me repeat that. Gratitude is the cornerstone of happiness, and happiness is the foundation on which you build your success.

Be grateful for everything in your life. The people. The opportunities. Your possessions. And even your disappointments, challenges, and failures. For it is all of these that add up to make you who you are at this very moment, and no matter how different you want to be in the future, I'm encouraging you to be grateful for the *you* you are today.

Get used to saying thank you. Say thank you to the cashier when you grab your morning paper or coffee. Say thank you to the stranger who holds the door for you. *Say thank you to your partner or spouse.* Say thank you to your children, neighbors, clients, and coworkers. Get used to saying thank you! Show your gratitude in your words and in your actions.

No matter how bad your day or week is going, be grateful for that day or week.

There have been so many times in my life when I could easily have gone down the path to self-pity, anger, and sadness. But instead, I lean on gratitude, and it always holds me up.

We become the result of the decisions we make. You can decide to live a life filled with gratitude.

Second is optimism.

Optimism is your most valuable tool to get you through the toughest, darkest times in your life. It is setting expectations of yourself. It is a form of confidence. Confidence in yourself and trust in others.

Through all the challenges in my life, and through the darkest times when it would have been easy to curl up, give up, and lose my way, it was always the optimism in my heart that cut through the dark clouds and kept me driving forward.

How you feel about something is a decision you make. Optimism is a choice.

We become the result of the decisions we make. Decide to be optimistic, no matter the situation. It might feel odd or awkward being optimistic during difficult times, but that's when you need your optimism the most.

Third is accountability.

You are the architect of your own life.

No one but you is responsible for your happiness. It is up to you, and only you, to create the vision for your future. It is your responsibility to set your goals, establish the actionable steps to achieve those goals, and be responsible for your decisions.

So, first and foremost, you need to be accountable to yourself. Create that good and honest picture of the person you want to be and hold yourself accountable to the behaviors, decisions, words, and actions that are consistent with that image of yourself. Without holding yourself accountable, then your goals and dreams are just wishes and hopes. Put on your adult pants and take responsibility for your own life.

But accountability goes beyond just yourself. You are accountable to others as well. You are accountable to your significant other and family; to your neighbors, friends, and community; to your coworkers and customers. When people trust your accountability, they trust you. People want to help people they trust. And your resilience is made so much stronger and easier when you are surrounded by people who want to help.

You become the result of the decisions you make. Be accountable.

These attitudes—gratitude, optimism, and accountability—are the backbones of strength that help me stand steadfast in the face of uncertainty and hard times.

Weave them into all your interactions along life's path. Sprinkle some respect and kindness into those interactions, and you will build strong relationships.

It is relationships that will pick you up when you are down. It is relationships that will celebrate your successes. And it is strong relationships that help you bounce back from difficult times, and propel you forward to achieve your dreams and goals.

Tested by time, these Pillars of Strength—gratitude, optimism, and accountability—have always held up my happiness and resilience, no matter what life throws at me. And probably just like you, life has thrown some shit my way.

In 2014, just months after our dad died, my oldest brother revealed his diagnosis of pancreatic cancer. He was a brilliant trauma surgeon and fought so hard. There was even a time when we thought he might be part of that 4 or 5 percent who survive this devastating disease. With the aid of our sister and one of my other brothers, he even flew halfway across the country in May 2015 to surprise me by attending a speech I was giving. Then things changed quickly, and we lost Carl Valenziano on August 24, 2015.

As a family, we were stunned. Losing our dad was difficult but an expected milestone as he was almost ninety. Our family's genes consistently demonstrated that we lived to be around ninety, so the loss of our oldest sibling in his early sixties was a huge kick to the gut. Our own mortality was suddenly in our consciousness.

Then the truly unfathomable occurred. Less than two months later, on October 20, my second-oldest brother told me he was in the hospital and had been diagnosed with leukemia. He was feeling healthy and was golfing two days earlier and playing tennis three days before that. On

October 19, he had the blood test he had semiannually because of the cholesterol medicine he was taking. He owned a manufacturing company and was a hard-driving, busy man who would stop in a heartbeat to give you the shirt off his back. In the midst of that busy Monday, his doctor phoned and told him to get to the hospital immediately and to be sure to not cut himself. His blood no longer had the ability to clot and stop the bleeding. How quickly our fragile lives can change.

Phil Valenziano died only seven weeks later, on December 12, 2015.

In 111 days, this world lost two powerhouse human beings, and our family was devastated. In such a short period, we went from a family of seven to a family of four, with the haze of Alzheimer's making it difficult for our mom to comprehend why her beloved husband and two of her sons were no longer around.

As the youngest of the five siblings, I looked to my older brothers and sister as my guiding beacons. It took some time to accept that two of my heroes were gone. This sudden change to my world left me feeling empty and lost.

If you learn nothing else from this book, please learn that life is fragile. Be grateful for this very moment and for the loved ones in your life. It can all change suddenly and without notice.

One month after burying Phil in New Jersey, the unbelievable happened yet again. While my wife and I were on a desperately needed vacation in Florida, my mother-in-law was on her daily walk through her California retirement community when she was struck by a drunk driver. She died after five days in a coma.

We were emotionally and physically exhausted. It seemed like we had been doing nothing but flying around the country, visiting hospitals, planning funerals, and saying goodbyes. In only four and a half months, our world had been turned completely upside down. Under the weight of these very dark clouds, it could have been easy to crumble and lose my way. But my Pillars of Strength were there to hold me up.

It was my optimism that kept slicing through the darkness and driving me forward. Reminding me that I could get through this tragic period in a positive way. My optimism kept my life on track despite the immense pain and loss. It was my accountability that helped me decide how to behave.

When I took my time to grieve, especially regarding my two brothers, rather than focusing on the sadness and the void in my life, I thought about how truly grateful I was, and still am, to have had these two beautiful people in my life. There is nothing wrong with sadness. It is important to feel it and own the sadness. But it is okay to give yourself permission to look to the future. It is okay to give yourself permission to be resilient. It is okay to give yourself permission to be happy. It is okay to let your gratitude outshine, and eventually even swallow up, your sorrow.

My inner movie played a role here too. It brought my words and actions into focus within the fog of tragedy. I rolled my inner movie to picture myself coming through this horrible time first and foremost in a way that would make my brothers proud. I used my inner movie to picture the words and actions that would make me the best uncle I could possibly be for my eight nieces and nephews, who just lost their dads. I pictured being the best sibling I could be to my remaining brother and sister, recognizing their struggles would differ from my own. I pictured how I could be most present for my two sisters-in-law, who were now suddenly widows. I pictured myself being the best spouse and in-law I could possibly be, for my wife and her family did not even get to say goodbye to their mother.

We become the result of the decisions we make. Decide to elevate your resilience on the three Pillars of Strength—gratitude, optimism, and accountability—and you will get through anything in life.

SCENE 5

Get the Heck
Out of Your Own Way!

As humans, we are complex mixtures of emotions, thoughts, ego, intellect, history, family, and multiple frames of reference. We are ever-changing, dynamic beings. And we can be stubborn. We each have inner obstacles that can get in the way of achieving our goals or building the relationships we desire, obstacles like defensiveness, apathy, arrogance, and insecurity. You can use your inner movie to view your behaviors and identify the obstacle and then rewrite the scene to literally see yourself differently, without that obstacle hindering your progress.

Here's how I did exactly this. The obstacle for me was insecurity, and it showed its ugly head when I bought my first white cane. There are two reasons I needed the cane. First, it indicates to others that I cannot see. If you don't know about my lack of eyesight, I appear completely "normal." If you waved to me from across the street, I'd appear arrogant and standoffish when I didn't return the wave—but I truly never saw you! I'm sure this happened far more times than I realize. In one case, a new neighbor in Minneapolis had waved or walked by me a number of times without me acknowledging her. At a BBQ months later, I told her a bit about myself, including the fact that I couldn't see. Her response was priceless when she quietly said, "I'm so glad to hear that." Not the typical response I get when I tell someone I can't see! But I understood completely.

My wife and I recently moved across the country, and something similar happened in our new neighborhood. Lori and I have our morning coffee and conversation on our front porch, waving or saying hello to our neighbors as they go by. Apparently one of those neighbors often waved to me when I was out there alone, but she never got a wave back. She commented to another neighbor that "he's not very friendly, but his wife seems very nice." So, you can understand why my having the white cane to identify myself as not being able to see can alter first impressions about me for the better.

After identification, the second reason for the white cane is navigation. I was having trouble navigating sidewalks, curbs, public stairways, and other obstacles. I also started bumping into oncoming pedestrians who, not knowing about my lack of sight, probably thought I was drunk. It was time to use a cane to help me get around a bit more safely.

I bought it with the best of intentions, but when it arrived, I immediately shoved it to the back of the closet, not to be touched for a long time. My response was visceral. I was afraid of the stigma. I was scared of what people would think and say. I was terrified this meant my sight was disappearing rapidly, which it was.

And then it happened. I was in my neighborhood hardware store and, with item in hand, was making my way to the cashier. I never saw the young woman standing at the end of the aisle. I was walking at a confident clip when I crashed squarely into her, knocking her backward where she fell into the corner of a metal display rack. I could not see the look on her face, but I sure did hear the shock and anger in her voice. This happened because I was insecure about carrying a damn piece of fiberglass. I was humiliated.

This clearly was not the kind of person I pictured myself being. Something needed to change. Again, that something was me.

Later, at home, I sat with my eyes closed, rolling my inner movie and reviewing that horrible scene that just occurred. I cringed when I saw that guy, up on my imaginary movie screen, crashing into that woman. I asked myself why this happened, and the answer was simple: I was not carrying my cane. Had I been, she would have known I was visually impaired. And I would have been walking more cautiously, tapping the cane out ahead of me to feel shelves, displays, and, yes, others' feet. Insecurity was getting in the way of me being the person I wanted to be.

So, I rolled my inner movie again and started to see myself differently. I visualized myself holding my white cane and being comfortable with it in my hands. I pictured myself walking my neighborhood and doing so with confidence. I used my imagination to anticipate the questions and comments I'd hear from neighbors and shop owners, as almost none of them knew I was going blind. By anticipating their questions and comments, I was prepared to respond comfortably.

With this new, confident image of myself in mind, I grabbed my cane, walked the neighborhood, and interacted with neighbors and strangers alike. I was so pleasantly surprised by humanity. It went so well. I removed the obstacle of insecurity and replaced it with confidence by exercising my imagination and literally seeing myself differently. Today, I am more uncomfortable when I don't have my cane.

I'm both lucky and grateful that the young woman in the store did not get hurt. It is not lost on me that she could have been seriously injured. This momentary scene of my life could have turned out so much worse.

Reflection Question

What obstacles are getting in your way of building important relationships or achieving your goals? What change have you been putting off?

Jot down two things you'd like to accomplish, professionally or personally, and identify the obstacles that may be preventing you from doing so. Insecurity, apathy, defensiveness, arrogance, and ego are common obstacles that are inside all of us. Be honest with yourself. It could be easy to rationalize reasons other than insecurity or other obstacles as the roadblock. If you say your obstacle is "I don't know how or don't have the knowledge or skill," then ask yourself what is stopping you from gaining that knowledge or learning that skill. If you say "a lack of time" is your obstacle, then assess the importance of the goal and reprioritize your schedule. Again, address these points for each goal:

What I want to accomplish
My internal obstacle that's preventing me

Is it time for you to start seeing yourself differently? Use your inner movie as a powerful tool to design your future and navigate the change required to get you there.

SCENE 6

Life Is a Balancing Act

To stay at the top of our game, we all need an amount of uncertainty in our life to keep ourselves motivated. But what is the right amount? Too much uncertainty may mean you're frazzled and worried more often than not. Too much uncertainty may be affecting your sleep, your attention, and your mood. But too little uncertainty in your life could mean you're complacent, unalert, and uninspired. Truth is, this not only varies person to person but also varies from topic to topic within one's life.

My Balanced-Uncertainty Index is the range of how you are feeling, from being completely comfortable, certain, and satisfied, to being uncomfortable, uncertain, and unsatisfied.

By answering a few questions, you will indicate your current position relative to what I call the Uncertainty Sweet Spot. The gap between your answers and the Sweet Spot is your personal opportunity to convert uncertainty to growth and accomplishment. It's your opportunity to be in better charge of your life.

The Sweet Spot is my unscientific favored point of balance between stagnation and achievement. Stagnation from anxiety, insecurity, or inflexibility. Achievement through confidence, action, and resilience.

The Sweet Spot is when you are feeling a good balance between complacency and your sense of drive for more and to be better. People have different personalities and thresholds, so everyone's Sweet Spot will differ slightly, but this will act as an indicator and get you thinking differently.

Your Sweet Spot is a feeling, one of cautious contentment. Kind of like "I'm okay for now, but I want more. And in the meantime, I'm going to stay really alert, aware, and inspired."

Exercise

Let's find your Balanced-Uncertainty Index now. Following is a list of ten Personal Reflection Points. These are general areas of your life to contemplate.

___ Your health
___ Your finances
___ Your personal relationships
___ Your job performance
___ Your job level and professional advancement
___ Your work relationships

___ Community involvement

___ Lifelong learning

___ Volunteerism

___ Spirituality

Using 1 through 10, indicate how you are currently feeling about each of these Personal Reflection Points. Are you where you want to be? Are you satisfied with your accomplishments? Can you perceive yourself doing more or being better?

Very low worries, doubts, or concerns   **Very high** worries, doubts, or concerns

A ① means you have very low or no worries, concerns, or doubts. You are comfortable or satisfied with your accomplishments, at this moment, in this Personal Reflection Point.

A ⑩ means you have a very high level of worry, doubt, or concern. You are not comfortable or satisfied with your accomplishments, at this moment, in this Personal Reflection Point.

Keep your future in mind. Although this exercise asks for how you're feeling at this moment, remember to include your future self in that calculation of your feelings at this moment. Is where you are today in the right trajectory with who you want to be tomorrow (both literally tomorrow and a distant tomorrow)?

Some of these Personal Reflection Points are multi-dimensional. For example, in any of the relationship-related Reflection Points, there are probably many people within your sphere. Focus your thinking on those relationships about which you are most worried or have high levels of uncertainty.

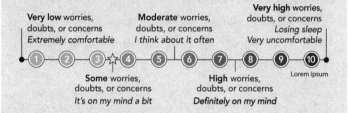

My personal Sweet Spot for each is generally around 3.5. Having some worries, doubts, and concerns keeps me alert and thinking. For me, this point of balance enables me to be calm and composed while still open to new ideas and opportunities. It keeps me problem-solving and inspired without being weighed down by too much worry or fear.

It is, of course, a sliding target, since your tolerance for discomfort, unsatisfaction, or uncertainty will vary from one Personal Reflection Point to another. When it comes to your finances, you may need great certainty and comfort compared to other areas of your life. But more important than the numeric value I happen to designate is the feeling I want to elicit. Happiness is a balance of many things in your life. It's finding your perfect amount of tension between comfortable stability and uncomfortable drive to grow and improve.

Some level of uncertainty is healthy for all of us. Assuming you're not a completely lazy couch potato, an increased dose of uncertainty in some areas of your life will keep you motivated, creative, and inquisitive. If you wrote a 1 for any of these Personal Reflection Points, then there's a chance you've become too complacent in this area of life. You might be overconfident and closed-minded to ideas and opportunities. Your blinders may be stifling your awareness of lurking conflicts or risks.

Striving for more in these areas of your life will translate to progress, satisfaction, and happiness. It will not just keep you at the top of your game—it will elevate your game.

For each Personal Reflection Point for which you marked a 1 or 2, jot down two goals, initiatives, wants, or desires you want to achieve. Then, for each of those, write down two or three action steps needed to make them happen.

For each Personal Reflection Point for which you marked a 5 or higher, think about what goals or accomplishments would help you feel more in control and give you more satisfaction within this area of your life. Write them down. Then think about what is holding you back. Are you lacking a skill or knowledge? Are you fearful of something? Write these down.

There is nothing wrong with starting small. As you

establish your goals, think about your level of control and the predictability of the outcome. Controllability and predictability factor heavily into your feelings of stress or uncertainty and can fuel feelings of insecurity. If you want to start small, set goals where you have some or high control and the outcome is more predictable. Goals or initiatives where you have little control and predictability is low may move your needle the wrong way on the Balanced-Uncertainty Index.

An area of psychology called industrial organizational psychology has focused on work stress and effectiveness. These professionals have identified controllability and predictability as playing a central role in issues of stress. I believe these two concepts contribute greatly to feelings of anxiety and uncertainty. So, as you challenge yourself and set your goals—especially goals within the more "personal" Personal Reflection Points—be sure to give some consideration to your ability to control and predict.

Don't sell yourself short. There is absolutely nothing wrong with some unpredictability and some lack of control. This may cause you to "worry productively," which may lead you to more thorough thinking and development of actionable plans that are more effective and successful. Find the right balance for you.

Use this Balanced-Uncertainty Index every few months to glance at your life and trigger new opportunities to learn and grow. If we do not push ourselves to learn, grow, adapt, and change, then we are choosing complacency and may become rigid and resistant rather than open and adaptable. If we do not push ourselves to continually get comfortable being uncomfortable, then we're just playing a cameo role in life as it unfolds around us. We're letting life happen to us, rather than being in charge of our life. Of our future.

Be aware, assess situations large or small, and make good decisions. This puts you in charge of your future and a step ahead of uncertainty.

"Start where you are. Use what you have. Do what you can."

—Arthur Ashe

Dude, What Are You Doing?

What are you doing with your life?

Do you have purpose in your life? Do you have that thing that gets you out of bed every morning and gets you going? According to research reported in Dan Buettner's books about the Blue Zones—the areas around the world where people tend to live to one hundred years old—having purpose can add up to seven years to your life expectancy. Purpose is that important for happiness and health.

Finding the reason for your existence can be difficult. Some people discover it at a young age, while others don't find it until much later in life. But this does not have to be a super-heavy and daunting task. If you struggle with this question of your "life's purpose," maybe think of it more in terms of what it is you like to do that's meaningful, has a positive impact, and makes you feel good.

For many years I did not exactly know my purpose. I naturally figured it was simply to be a good person. To be good to my family and friends. To do my best to succeed in business, and that was about it.

I always observed my dad asking people, "What can I do to help?" so it became natural for me to do the same. It feels quite good to offer someone your help and deliver on that offer. You can't always deliver the desired result, but you feel good knowing that you tried.

When I owned my company in the health industry, I assumed my purpose was to help people feel better and stay healthier. We were very good at it, and in general, I enjoyed the work. But I had a huge awakening when my brothers died. Suddenly my own mortality was front and center in my mind. It became very real to me that none of us know when our last breath will come. It quickly became clear to me that, as long as you can financially afford it, you've got to be doing exactly what it is you want to be doing—*now*. I'm not saying a twenty-seven-year-old should abandon their first job to go ski, surf, or travel the world. I am saying that at some point, maybe in your fifties, you should take an inventory of your life. Evaluate your financial position and decide if you are truly doing what you want to be doing with your time. With your life.

In addition to the tragedies with my family members, my sight was disappearing rapidly. More and more work was being put on my assistant's plate. Twice, while carrying heavy items perched on my shoulder, I came close to tripping on unseen obstacles and falling down flights of stairs with our customer walking just steps in front of me. My work tasks were becoming more and more in conflict with who I was becoming. My enjoyment and satisfaction were dwindling. So, I sold my company.

After taking some time off, I embarked on something much more in concert with who I was and started my new adventure as a public speaker. I had given many speeches to large audiences for charitable causes but had not thought about making it my profession. I'm glad I did.

An opportunity serendipitously dropped into my lap, and I ran with it. This first professional talk turned into an award for Best Personal Development Program within Young Presidents Organization (YPO), thanks to the passion and energy of my new friend Jayna. (Thank you for believing in me, Jayna!) This resulted in me giving my talks across North America, Central America, South America, and Puerto Rico. I was a bit dazed by the flurry of bookings and overwhelmingly positive response to my events.

The flickers of my "purpose" were starting to brighten, but they truly came to light for me in Guayaquil, Ecuador. At the end of a talk, a woman with tears in her eyes came up to give me a huge hug, during which she whispered, "Thank you." Then she stepped back, held my shoulders, and said, "This is why you were put on this earth." She was facing some big challenges in her life and told me she now had a road map and felt inspired and hopeful. I gave her a few more words of encouragement, returned the hug, and whispered, "Thank you," right back to her.

I was humbled. I had heard these kinds of comments many times, but there was something about this woman's expression that struck me deeply. Listen to those around you. Hear what they appreciate about you. You might just find the threads of your purpose in their words.

This sense of purpose can evolve as you go through life. It will be shaped by your experiences and the people with whom you surround yourself. But it is critical to establish what's important to you. What do you value? What issues, groups, or topics are important to you? Examples are:

Family and friends
Community and society
Teaching
Nature and environment
Social justice
Helping the less fortunate

The list is endless, and certainly you will value more than just one.

Reflection Question

Jot down three issues or initiatives that are important to you. It doesn't matter the reason why they are important to you—those reasons can be as numerous as the stars. You may have lost a dear loved one and want to live a life that would make them proud. You may have witnessed an event that gave you a new perspective on something that needs to change. You may have just always felt called toward a particular topic and not know why.

Your purpose may change over time, but it will always orbit around your core values. Having purpose in your life will keep you true to your values, and having values will keep you true to your purpose. A sense of purpose in your life will minimize distractions and make it easier to stay focused and passionate about your goals and life in general. Without a sense of purpose as your beacon, your actions, goals, and accomplishments might be more haphazard and less fulfilling.

Sometimes standing up and being true to yourself in front of the world can be scary. It takes courage to be your authentic self. It's okay to have some fear; out of your fear shines your bravery and courage. Stand tall. Be proud. Find your purpose and be the person you want to be.

SCENE 8

You Are Your Own Brand

The best thing you can build is your name. You are your brand. What are you writing into the next scene of your life to make it the best it can possibly be? What simple change have you been putting off? There is no time like the present! There is no time like the present to live in a way that outsmarts the uncertainty that comes with life. By knowing who you are, who you want to be, and making prudent, thoughtful decisions, you can balance the uncertainty in your life and keep yourself moving away from anxiety and always toward accomplishment. Use the Balanced-Uncertainty Index in Scene 6 to help you view uncertainty as opportunity, so you can turn it to your advantage and flourish. I'll tell you how a friend of mine approached this.

She had worried her whole life about her lack of accomplishments, but she was doing nothing about her concerns. She was playing only a cameo role as life unfolded around her. She was stagnating and filling herself with anxiety. We talked about what she wanted to accomplish, who she wanted to become, how she wanted to feel, and what it would take to achieve her goals and dreams. She reflected on the Balanced-Uncertainty Index and realized she desired more balance and growth in her personal health, personal finances, and professional achievement. She happily recognized that becoming a health instructor would not only be achieving her dream but would bring her life into balance. She spoke with people who could guide her, and she methodically worked through the steps of her education and certifications. And the small network of relationships she built helped her quickly find the type of employment she was seeking. She replaced her anxiety with accomplishment and greatly enhanced her happiness by doing so.

You are on the cusp of your own greatness. Consider this moment a new beginning. A fresh start. An opportunity to examine your life and determine your brand. How will you define your brand?

Reflection Question

What are the seven words you want people to use when describing you?

Now select five people from different areas of your life and ask them the following question: If you were giving my eulogy and could only use seven words, what seven words would you use to describe me?

Compare their list of words with your own to understand how well you are communicating your brand. This will indicate how well your outward behavior, words, and actions align with what you want people to think about you. If they don't align well, you may have some soul-searching to do in order to bring more congruency to the person you want to be and the person you are being.

Who do you want to be? How are you defining and improving your personal brand? What do you want people to think or feel when they think of you?

If you can picture your new self up on that big imaginary movie screen and believe in yourself, then you will slowly but surely become that person. A happier person. And that smile on your face, jump in your step, and proud happiness in your heart will only grow.

Vision, awareness, and good decisions eclipse uncertainty. Vivid imagination and mental toughness eclipse uncertainty. Seeing yourself differently is your starting point.

SCENE 9

Go for It!

Years ago, my dad and I were talking on the phone about a company I was considering starting. He asked lots of questions to make sure I was thinking through the risks and challenges, and he had some helpful ideas and sage advice.

A few days later an envelope arrived in the mail. Inside, scribbled in Dad's distinctive handwriting, were three words: "Go for it!" This may sound trite, but it takes more than just having an idea of what you want to have happen; you need to act, step by step, to put your ideas in motion.

Ultimately, you are the architect of your life. This is your journey. This is your opportunity to create an even better version of yourself.

So, if you are a parent and want to be better in some area of your parenting, then envision yourself being that way. Remove the obstacles to your greatness and evolve to become that parent.

If you are indifferent about work and count down the minutes until five o'clock or Friday, then I urge you to replace that apathy with care. You are important in so many ways; see yourself that way. You will be much happier gaining that value out of each day rather than just letting your limited time pass you by.

If you're comfortable and complacent at work, then there's a good chance you have some skills that need sharpening. What are they? Which of your Personal Reflection Points need your attention?

YOUR HEALTH

How is your weight, blood pressure, and cholesterol?
Do you eat well?
Are you getting enough exercise per week?
When was your last physical?

YOUR FINANCES

How much debt do you have? What is your plan and time-
table to eliminate your debt?
Are you adding to savings each month?
How many months or years can you go without an income?
Do you have a financial advisor?

YOUR PERSONAL RELATIONSHIPS

If you want one, are you in a loving relationship?
Do you have a group of friends you enjoy being with and
can count on? It is so important to surround ourselves
with a diverse group of good people we can learn from,

laugh with, and count on. It is okay to "release" people from your life if they hold you back or regularly drain your energy rather than add to your spirit and mood. It is normal for people to move in and out of our lives.

YOUR JOB PERFORMANCE

What skills should you be sharpening?

What are your strengths?

What is something new you can learn that will help improve your job performance?

YOUR JOB LEVEL AND PROFESSIONAL ADVANCEMENT

Do you want more out of your profession?

What are a few good next avenues in your career development?

What do you need to do or learn to position yourself properly for these opportunities?

Who can help you pursue these career opportunities? (We all need people!)

YOUR WORK RELATIONSHIPS

Do you have good relationships with the people who can help you succeed at your job?

Do you get along with the people above you, below you, and around you?

YOUR COMMUNITY INVOLVEMENT

Do you know your neighbors?

Are you somehow involved with your community?

Do you make a point to know people who are different from you?

LIFELONG LEARNING

Is there something you want to be learning? Maybe a language, music, art, or history?

If not a specific topic to learn, do you keep your brain active with reading, puzzles, or games?

VOLUNTEERISM

Are you giving of your time, energy, and talent?

SPIRITUALITY

Have you contemplated something beyond yourself?

By first picturing the new behaviors you want to recognize in yourself, it is truly possible to initiate difficult and important change in your life. Here's how I did this with my own personal health. I wanted to be perceived as a person who takes good care of himself mentally and physically. I realized the person I was being was not consistent with that vision of myself, so I took this action:

1. I decided I wanted to lose weight without going on some fad diet. I knew this should also have a positive effect on my blood pressure and cholesterol. I rolled my inner movie and pictured myself after losing the weight. I envisioned my proud happiness upon achieving my goal.

2. I identified a few dietary changes I'd make each day. I gave

nothing up completely but did shift the balance of what I ate and drank to be healthier and in line with my goal.

3. To conjure the discipline I'd need to be successful, I visualized myself going through each day with this goal in mind. I pictured my behavior at home, at parties, and at restaurants to predetermine how I'd behave when ordering food and drinks or when someone put a bowl of chips in front of me. I committed to myself.

4. I set aside time each week for light exercise and committed to making it a priority.

5. I set an achievable goal and gave myself a deadline by which I'd reach my goal.

6. To measure the quantifiable results, I went to a doctor and then again after sixty days. Here is what I achieved:

- I lost five inches off my waist.
- My cholesterol dropped by twenty-nine points.
- I lost thirteen pounds.
- My blood pressure lowered by thirty points.

I used my inner movie to achieve my goal by simply seeing myself differently. I saw myself being more disciplined and making smart choices—always keeping my goal in mind. Change is difficult. It takes mental toughness to be the person you aspire to be. It takes energy and time. It takes commitment. But you are worth it. Your brand is worth it. Your evolving happiness is worth it.

Taking charge of your future is worth it. Commit to it. Commit to yourself!

Life Is Cyclical, and You Are Not Exempt

But you can spread out the cycles and enjoy the ride! You age. Things change. You adapt and get comfortable. You age again.

You pursue your goals. You take on the uncertainty and accomplish what you want. You get comfortable and decide to pursue new goals. As you should!

And no matter who you are, shit just happens in life. It causes uncertainty, anxiety, and maybe fear. You are resilient, deal with it, and bounce back. Then shit happens again.

The key is to maximize stability in your life by lengthening the time between cycles. The more alert, aware, and inspired you remain, the less frequent these cycles will be, resulting in more stability and more happiness and less time feeling frazzled. And if the unfathomable rapid succession of bad events occurs in your life, being grounded in yourself will help you stand steadfast and tall even in the darkest of times.

Use the Balanced-Uncertainty Index as a tool to keep you aware and inspired. It will help you identify your personal opportunities for growth and progress. Disappointments are inevitable, so keep your resilience energized by filling your life with the three Pillars of Strength: gratitude, optimism, and accountability. As Albert Einstein said, "Failure is success in progress."

Today's new environment, spurred on by a pandemic, may be ushering in a new cycle and calling upon you to create the next leg of your journey. It has for me. Since selling my company and embarking on the adventure of public speaking, I've had the exciting privilege of speaking to audiences across multiple continents. Being on stage telling my story is exactly what I want to be doing. It gives me great energy and enjoyment. It is in concert with who I am rather than in conflict. But because of COVID-19, all of my bookings for live appearances in 2020 and much of 2021 dried up. Like so many Americans, I quickly went from a busy schedule and good income to nothing! COVID-19 forced me to reinvent myself, again.

Time to pivot and be resilient. Time to rewrite the script for the next scene of my life.

The cycle has returned, and once again, I'm facing uncertainty and insecurity. As a blind public speaker, the thought of delivering engaging virtual events through a camera I cannot see, to an audience whose energy I cannot feel, is completely unsettling and uncomfortable. But to make the storyline I'm envisioning come true, and to create the impact and life that I want, it's critical that I accept the risks and rewards that change offers, and step forward to adapt, learn, and innovate.

I invite you to do the same. Let's journey into the future together and go for it!

SCENE 11

One Last Thought

And one last story.

We are often stunned or shocked by troubling situations and immediately default to thinking the worst. This can be mood-altering, crippling, and unhealthy. Some situations are horrible and do require our immediate and full attention. But sometimes things are not nearly as bad as they appear, affording us the opportunity to take a deep breath and enjoy the beautiful feeling of gratefulness. Tuck these moments of good fortune in the back pocket of your memory to be smiled about later.

Some years ago I was climbing a Colorado 14er (one of the state's fifty-eight mountain peaks reaching higher than fourteen thousand feet) with my friend Jeff and his good buddy Jay. The final push to the peak was a long and steep field of giant boulders as far as the eye could see. Normally sighted people could take a couple steps on each giant rock and jump to the next one. But with only a sliver of peripheral vision at my disposal, this became quite difficult and dangerous. So, after a while, I changed my approach and slowly made the ascent on my hands and knees. We were well above the trees, the sun was bright, and the boulders were honey in color, creating an incredibly bright "bowl" in which we were tiny little specs scaling upward. People who are losing their sight to diseases of the retina are typically very photosensitive, and the bright surroundings were killing me despite my high-quality sunglasses. I was visually exhausted and struggling to keep my eyes open. I was physically exhausted from crawling up the steep incline. My shins, knees, and hands were scraped and bruised. I was emotionally spent. Jeff and Jay were so kind and kept their pace slow to stick with me. But with another five hundred or six hundred vertical feet remaining to the summit, I decided to stop. My complete exhaustion was simply making it too dangerous. I told Jeff I'd wait right there for the couple hours it would take him and Jay to reach the top, enjoy the peak, and get back down to me. He agreed, and they went on their way. I put on my rain gear to protect me from the brutal sun, drank some water, got as comfortable as I could, and fell asleep.

Despite being balanced on an uneven giant rock on a steep mountainside, I slept deeply. When I awoke, however, I experienced the absolutely scariest moment of my life. I cautiously stood up, stretched, and turned around to gaze up the mountain. And that was when, out of my sliver of vision, I spotted it. Silhouetted against the bright rocks a few hundred feet up from me was a mountain lion! Its tail was slowly swinging, and from what I figured, its eyes were fixed on me. Contemplating its next meal, I presumed.

I screamed Jeff's name into the mountaintop wind and quickly dropped to my belly and reached between the massive boulders in search of weapons. I was not about to become dinner without a fight. I gathered softball- and football-size rocks and set my arsenal in front of me. Back on my feet, I frantically scanned the mountainside to get my carnivorous attacker back in my peripheral sights, all the while screaming Jeff's name.

Jeff was finally able to hear me and screamed back, "What?" As loud as I could, I yelled, "MOUNTAIN LION!"

My heart was racing. My eyes were scanning back and forth quickly, trying to find Jeff and keep my predator's swinging tail in sight. I could not find Jeff. Turned out there was a good reason; Jeff and the mountain lion were one and the same! The tail I saw swinging was a long strap hanging from Jeff's pack. The dark silhouette against the golden brightness of the sun-drenched rocks appeared to be a lion—especially since Jeff could not hear me over the wind and did not immediately reply to my frantic calls for help. And since you can't focus your peripheral vision, and I had no central vision, there was no possible way for me to see that it was Jeff. But I'm damn glad it was!

My heart slowed, we had a good laugh, and the three of us slowly descended the mountain back to our camp.

When I am in difficult circumstances wrought with uncertainty, ones that may even appear to be dire, the memory of this mountainside experience flashes through my mind as a reminder that things may not be as bad as they seem. And for the most part they are not. Uncertainty will never disappear, nor should you want it to. But I hope the tools, wisdom, and stories in this book inspire you to outsmart uncertainty, go after your goals and dreams, and create your best life amid chaos and anxiety. I truly want you to live a wonderfully happy life like the one I enjoy.

Roll the Credits

First and foremost, I want to thank Lori, my wife, for her unending support and love. It is not easy to be married to me, never mind the added difficulty of being married to a blind person. Thank you so much, sweetheart! I love you.

To my parents, Mae and Frank, and brothers, Carl and Phil, who have let their spirits fly free and are dancing with the angels. I will always cherish my unending gratitude, respect, and love for each of you.

To the memories of Drs. Paul Ocken and Eliot Berson. Dr. Ocken, in Warren, New Jersey, was the first to diagnose me. I was a scared teenager, but he treated me like an adult. The respect and kindness he showed helped establish my attitude and set my life on a course for success. Words and actions matter. Dr. Berson, in Cambridge, Massachusetts, was brutally honest with me during my college years. His respectful honesty helped me make decisions that shaped where I lived and what I did.

I am grateful for them both.

To my sister, Angela, brother, Frank, and our whole big family: thanks for all your enthusiastic support of all my crazy endeavors! I love and appreciate each of you.

Thank you to my beta readers and casual contributors, whose comments, questions, and ideas helped me more than they realize.

And many thanks to my wonderful editor, Kristin Thiel, and book designer/publishing guru, Vinnie Kinsella, whose energy, passion, and talent truly made this project far better than I could have ever accomplished without them. We all need people!

Get Your Tickets for the Next Show

Mark Valenziano is a former corporate executive and entrepreneur who sold his successful company to follow his passion: educating and inspiring people to truly be in charge of their future, rather than just letting life happen to them. Mark's engaging storytelling ability leverages his unique perspective as someone who has journeyed from being sighted to being blind. Informed by this transition starting when he was fifteen, he has developed uniquely powerful programs on resilience, inclusion, and managing uncertainty. He teaches the principles and tools that help organizations and individuals not only navigate change but use change to create positive benefits and opportunities. An energetic and entertaining speaker, Mark will engage your staff, team, or conference from the moment he walks on stage until his closing point.

"I've known Mark for years and have seen him in action. His message will inspire and entertain. Prepare to be amazed and energized!"

—Frank Vascellaro, news anchor, CBS News/ WCCO-TV, Minneapolis–St. Paul, MN

"We were so fortunate to have Mark Valenziano speak at our corporate event. Over the past ten years, we have had various inspirational speakers. None comes close to Mark. He is passionate, eloquent, and gets his message across to the entire audience. After Mark's talk, many attendees told me how much they enjoyed the talk, both professionally and personally. I highly recommend Mark to speak at any organizational or corporate event. Give your people this gift!"

—Karen Holzberg, president, KH International, Atlanta, GA

"Mark did an inclusivity workshop for two hundred of our employees. The feedback was incredible! Several people remarked that this was one of our best programs ever! His authentic style and moving message touches people's hearts. During his talk, people were so attentive and engaged that they were physically leaning in. Several days later people were still talking about what they took away from the event; now, that's real impact! I highly recommend Mark Valenziano as a speaker/facilitator!"

—Loretta Menke, associate director,
Organization Development & Learning, UCare,
Minneapolis–St. Paul, MN

Please visit www.markvalenziano.com to learn more about Mark's experiential workshops, unique dinner events, and his keynotes. What differentiates Mark is his ability to bring his amazing story to life in a way that resonates uniquely with each audience member. His dynamic presentations will change the audience's view on life. People will be motivated to embrace change. The vision they have for their future will be clear, positive, and achievable. After all, Mark knows a thing or two about living with uncertainty…and flourishing!

For availability and to have Mark speak at your event, please contact him directly at info@markvalenziano.com. Or fill out the form at: https://markvalenziano.com/contact.

CPSIA information can be obtained
at www.ICGtesting.com
Printed in the USA
BVHW040530060821
613736BV00011B/853